Make Your Own Own Cookies

LOVE FOOD™

First published in 2013
LOVE FOOD is an imprint of Parragon Books Ltd

Parragon,
Chartist House,
15–17 Trim Street,
Bath, BA1 1HA, UK

Copyright © Parragon Books Ltd 2013

LOVE FOOD and the accompanying heart device is a registered trade mark of Parragon Books Ltd
Australia, the UK, USA, India and the EU.

www.parragon.com/lovefood

ISBN:978-1-78186-404-3

Printed in China

New photography by Clive Streeter
New home economy by Sally Streeter
New recipes by Angela Drake
Edited by Fiona Biggs
Introduction by Angela Drake

Notes for the Reader
This book uses both metric and imperial measurements. Follow the same units of measurement
throughout; do not mix metric and imperial. All spoon measurements are level: teaspoons are assum
to be 5 ml, and tablespoons are assumed to be 15 ml. Unless otherwise stated, milk is assumed to be
full fat, eggs and individual vegetables are medium, and pepper is freshly ground black pepper. Unle
otherwise stated, all root vegetables should be washed and peeled prior to using.

The times given are an approximate guide only. Preparation times differ according to the technique
used by different people and the cooking times may also vary from those given. Optional ingredients
variations or serving suggestions have not been included in the time calculations.

Recipes using raw or very lightly cooked eggs should be avoided by infants, the elderly, pregnant wo
convalescents and anyone suffering from an illness. Pregnant and breastfeeding women are advised t
avoid eating peanuts and peanut products. Sufferers from nut allergies should be aware that some of
ready-made ingredients used in the recipes in this book may contain nuts. Always check the packagi
before use. Vegetarians should be aware that some of the ready-made ingredients used in the recipe
this book may contain animal products. Always check the packaging before use.

Contents

IT'S COOKIE TIME!

There's nothing more delicious and comforting than eating a freshly baked home-made cookie and nothing more satisfying than baking them yourself! Cookies are so easy to make; with just a few simple and inexpensive ingredients, they can be whipped up for a mid-morning snack or afternoon treat.

The added beauty of home-baked cookies is that you can customise them for any occasion just by using shaped cookie cutters or adding simple decorations. From Valentine's Day to Halloween, birthdays and baby showers, there's a cookie to suit any celebration.

EQUIPMENT

To make the majority of cookies in this book you'll only need general baking equipment that you will probably already have in your kitchen – scales, measuring spoons, mixing bowls, sieves, wooden and metal spoons, a large and small rolling pin and a selection of knives, including a palette knife. For baking the cookies, a couple of sturdy baking sheets are essential as well as a supply of baking paper and at least two wire cooling racks.

To make shaped cookies you'll need a range of cookie cutters. As well as the basic fluted and plain, round and square-shaped cutters that you may already have, you can also choose from a huge variety of shapes for any event or occasion from gingerbread men to flowers and animals. Don't be tempted to buy cutters that are too intricate as they can be fiddly to use.

For decorating cookies, disposable plastic piping bags are easy to use or you can make your own paper piping bags from greaseproof paper. A selection of small plain and fluted piping nozzles will be handy too. If you want to be a bit more adventurous you can invest in a cookie press, which will stamp out a soft buttery cookie dough into a variety of shapes before baking.

ROYAL ICING

Makes 1 quantity (approx 200 g/7 oz)

2 tbsp beaten egg white

175 g/6 oz icing sugar, sifted

water or lemon juice, if needed

1. Place the egg white in a bowl and add a little of the sugar. Beat with a wooden spoon or hand-held electric mixer until smooth.

2. Gradually beat in the remaining sugar to make a smooth, thick icing that holds soft peaks. For a thinner, spreadable icing, beat in a few drops of water to get the required consistency.

To colour the icing - using a cocktail stick, add a little liquid or paste food colouring and mix thoroughly.

Rolled & Cut-out Cookies

These simple cookies have a firm, buttery dough which is rolled out to an even thickness before shapes are cut from the dough with a cookie cutter. From gingerbread men to Valentine heart cookies, these delicious treats are perfect for special occasions or to give as gifts.

Iced Stars

Ingredients

225 g/8 oz butter, softened

140 g/5 oz caster sugar

1 egg yolk, lightly beaten

½ tsp vanilla extract

280 g/10 oz plain flour

salt

To decorate

200 g/7 oz icing sugar

edible food colourings

silver and gold balls

hundreds and thousands

sugar sprinkles

sugar stars, hearts and flowers

desiccated coconut

1. Put the butter and sugar into a bowl and mix well until creamy. Beat in the egg yolk and vanilla extract. Sift in the f and a pinch of salt and mix to a firm dough. Lightly knead until smooth. Halve the dough, shape it into two balls, wrap clingfilm and chill in the refrigerator for 30–60 minutes.

2. Preheat the oven to 190°C/375°F/Gas Mark 5. Line two baking sheets with baking paper.

3. Unwrap the dough and roll out between two sheets of ba paper to about 3 mm/⅛ inch thick. Stamp out 30 cookies w a star-shaped cutter, re-rolling the dough as necessary. Place the prepared baking sheets, spaced well apart and bake in th preheated oven for 10–15 minutes, until golden brown. Lea to cool on the baking sheets for a few minutes, then transfer cookies to wire racks to cool completely.

4. To decorate, sift the icing sugar into a bowl and stir in 1–2 tablespoons warm water until the mixture has the consistency of thick cream. Divide the icing among three to four bowls and add a few drops of your chosen food colourings to each. Leave the cookies on the racks and sprea the different coloured icings over them to the edges. Arrang silver and gold balls on top and/or sprinkle with hundreds a thousands, etc. If you like, coat desiccated coconut with edib food colouring in a contrasting colour and use to decorate. Leave to set.

3.

4.

Flower Gems

Makes 30   Prep Time 30 mins. plus chilling   Cook Time 10–12 mins.

Ingredients

225 g/8 oz butter, softened
140 g/5 oz caster sugar
1 egg yolk, lightly beaten
1 tsp lemon juice
280 g/10 oz plain flour
2 tbsp jasmine tea leaves
salt

To decorate

1 tbsp lemon juice
200 g/7 oz icing sugar
orange, pink, blue and yellow food colouring
orange, pink, blue and yellow sugar flowers

1. Put the butter and sugar into a bowl and mix well until creamy. in the egg yolk and lemon juice. Sift the flour and a pinch of salt, a the tea leaves and mix to a firm dough. Lightly knead until smooth Halve the dough, shape it into two balls, wrap in clingfilm and chil the refrigerator for 30–60 minutes.

2. Preheat the oven to 190°C/375°F/Gas Mark 5. Line two bakin sheets with baking paper.

3. Unwrap the dough and roll out the dough between two sheets of baking paper to about 3 mm/$^1/_8$ inch thick. Stamp out 30 flowers with a 5-cm/2-inch flower cutter, re-rolling the dough a necessary. Place on the prepared baking sheets, spaced well apart a bake in the preheated oven for 10–12 minutes, until golden brown. Leave to cool on the baking sheets for a few minutes, then transfer the cookies to wire racks to cool completely.

4. To decorate, mix the lemon juice with 1 tablespoon water in a bowl, then gradually stir in enough icing sugar to make a mixture consistency of thick cream. Divide the icing between four separate bowls and add a drop of different food colouring to each.

5. Leave the cookies on the racks. Spread the cookies with the diffe coloured icing and, once it's beginning to set, add a matching flowe the centre of each. Leave to set completely.

Valentine Heart Cookies

Makes 14   Prep Time 50 mins. plus chilling   Cook Time 12–15 mins.

Ingredients

100 g/3½ oz butter, softened,
plus extra for greasing

55 g/2 oz caster sugar

1 tsp finely grated lemon rind

1 egg yolk

200 g/7 oz plain flour,
for dusting

To decorate

1 quantity pink royal icing
(see page 5)

few drops of water

tube of white writing icing

1. Put the butter and sugar into a bowl and beat together until pale and creamy. Beat in the lemon rind and egg yolk. Sift in the flour and mix to a firm dough. Lightly knead until smooth, then wrap in clingfilm and chill in the refrigerator fo 30 minutes.

2. Preheat the oven to 180°C/350°F/Gas Mark 4. Grease tw baking sheets with butter.

3. Unwrap the dough and roll out on a lightly floured work surface to a thickness of 5 mm/¼ inch. Using a 7-cm/2¾-i heart-shaped cutter, stamp out 14 hearts, re-rolling the doug as necessary. Place on the prepared baking sheets, spaced we apart and bake in the preheated oven for 12–15 minutes, un golden. Leave to cool on the baking sheets for a few minutes then transfer to a wire rack to cool completely.

4. Spoon 3 tablespoons of the icing into a piping bag fitted with a fine nozzle and pipe an outline around each cookie. Slacken the remaining icing with a little water and spoon on the cookies, easing it to the piped edge with a teaspoon. Pip white polka dots onto the cookies with the white writing icin Leave to set.

1.

4.

Christmas Tree Cookies

Makes 16   Prep Time 45 mins.   Cook Time 10–15 mins.

Ingredients

225 g/8 oz plain flour, plus extra for dusting

2 tsp ground ginger

1/2 tsp bicarbonate of soda

55 g/2 oz butter, plus extra for greasing

3 tbsp golden syrup

70 g/2 1/2 oz soft light brown sugar

1 large egg yolk

To decorate

1 quantity green royal icing (see page 5)

tubes of red and yellow writing icing

1. Preheat the oven to 180°C/350°F/Gas Mark 4. Grease two baking sheets with butter. Sift the flour, ginger and bicarbonate of soda into a bowl and mix.

2. Put the butter, golden syrup and sugar into a saucepan and gently heat until syrupy. Add to the flour mixture with the egg yolk and mix to a firm dough. Lightly knead until smooth.

3. Roll out the dough on a lightly floured work surface to a thickness of 5 mm/1/4 inch. Using a 10-cm/4-inch Christmas tree-shaped cutter, cut out 16 trees, re-rolling the dough as necessary. Place on the prepared baking sheets, spaced well apart and bake in the preheated oven for 10–15 minutes until golden. Leave to cool on the baking sheets for a few minutes, then transfer to a wire rack to cool completely.

4. Beat a few drops of water into the icing to give a thick spooning consistency. Use a teaspoon to gently spread the icing on the cookies. Pipe decorations onto each iced tree with the tubes of red and yellow icing. Leave to set.

3.

4.

Sugar Cookies

Makes 20 | Prep Time 20 mins, plus chilling | Cook Time 10–12 mins.

Ingredients

115 g/4 oz butter, softened,
plus extra for greasing

55 g/2 oz caster sugar,
plus extra for sprinkling

1 tsp finely grated lemon rind

1 egg yolk

175 g/6 oz plain flour,
plus extra for dusting

1. Put the butter and sugar into a bowl and mix well until creamy. Beat in the lemon rind and egg yolk. Sift in the flour and mix to a firm dough. Lightly knead until smooth. Halve dough, shape it into two balls, wrap in clingfilm and chill in refrigerator for 1 hour.

2. Preheat the oven to 180°C/350°F/Gas Mark 4. Lightly grease two large baking sheets.

3. Unwrap the dough and roll out on a lightly floured work surface to a thickness of 5 mm/¼ inch. Using 7-cm/2¾-inch flower-shaped and heart-shaped cutters, stamp out 20 cookies re-rolling the dough as necessary. Place on the prepared baking sheets and space well apart. Sprinkle the cookies with the extra sugar and bake in the preheated oven for 10–12 minutes, or until pale gold in colour.

4. Leave to cool on the baking sheets for a few minutes, then transfer to a wire rack to cool completely.

Gingerbread Men

Makes 16   Prep Time 30 mins.   Cook Time 10–15 mins.

Ingredients

450 g/1 lb plain flour,
plus extra for dusting

2 tsp ground ginger

1 tsp bicarbonate of soda

115 g/4 oz butter,
plus extra for greasing

5 tbsp golden syrup

150 g/5½ oz soft light
brown sugar

1 large egg, beaten

To decorate

½ quantity royal icing
(see page 5)

48 candy-coated chocolate buttons

1. Preheat the oven to 180°C/350°F/Gas Mark 4. Grease two large baking sheets with butter. Sift the flour, ginger and bicarbonate of soda into a bowl and mix.

2. Put the butter, golden syrup and sugar into a saucepan and gently heat until syrupy. Add to the flour mixture together with the beaten egg and mix to a firm dough.

3. Roll out the dough on a lightly floured work surface to a thickness of 8 mm/³⁄₈ inch and, using a shaped cutter, stamp out 16 gingerbread men, re-rolling the dough as necessary. Place on the prepared baking sheets, spaced well apart and bake in the preheated oven for 10–15 minutes, until golden brown. Leave to cool on the baking sheets for a few minutes then transfer to a wire rack to cool completely.

4. Spoon the icing into a piping bag fitted with a fine nozzle and use to decorate the gingerbread men with faces and bow ties. Attach the chocolate buttons with a little of the icing. Leave to set.

3.

4.

Gingerbread Women

| Makes 16 | Prep Time 45 mins. | Cook Time 10–15 minutes |

Ingredients

450 g/1 lb plain flour,
plus extra for dusting

2 tsp ground ginger

1 tsp ground cinnamon

1 tsp bicarbonate of soda

115 g/4 oz butter,
plus extra for greasing

5 tbsp golden syrup

150 g/5½ oz soft light brown sugar

1 large egg, beaten

To decorate

350 g/12 oz pink ready-to-roll icing

icing sugar, for dusting

1 quantity pink royal icing
(see page 5)

silver balls

1. Preheat the oven to 180°C/350°F/Gas Mark 4. Grease two baking sheets with butter. Sift the flour, ginger, cinnamon and bicarbonate of soda into a bowl.

2. Put the butter, golden syrup and sugar into a saucepan and gently heat until syrupy. Add to the flour mixture together with the beaten egg and mix to a firm dough.

3. Roll out the dough on a lightly floured work surface to a thickness of 8 mm/⅜ inch and, using a gingerbread man-shaped cutter, stamp out 16 gingerbread men, re-rolling the dough as necessary. Place on the prepared baking sheets, spaced well apart and bake in the preheated oven for 10–15 minutes, until golden. Leave to cool on the baking sheets for a few minutes, then transfer to a wire rack to cool completely.

4. To decorate, thinly roll out the pink ready-to-roll icing on a work surface lightly dusted with icing sugar. Use the gingerbread man-shaped cutter to stamp out dresses (cutting away the head, feet and hands and trimming to a dress shape) and attach to the gingerbread men with a little of the royal icing. Press the silver balls into the pink icing to resemble buttons. Spoon the remaining royal icing into a piping bag fitted with a fine nozzle and use to pipe decorations on the cookies. Leave to set.

2.

3.

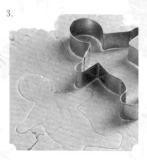

Drop Cookies

Made with a soft, sweet dough that's simply dropped onto
the baking sheets, these cookies are really quick and
easy to make — no chilling or shaping needed. Perfect
for an after-school treat, or to make at a moment's
notice for unexpected guests.

Chocolate Chip Cookies

Makes 30   Prep Time 15 mins.   Cook Time 10–12 mins.

Ingredients

175 g/6 oz plain flour

1 tsp baking powder

125 g/4½ oz soft margarine,
plus extra for greasing

85 g/3 oz light muscovado sugar

55 g/2 oz caster sugar

½ tsp vanilla extract

1 egg

125 g/4½ oz plain chocolate chips

1. Preheat the oven to 190°C/375°F/Gas Mark 5. Lightly grease two baking sheets.

2. Put all of the ingredients in a large mixing bowl and beat until well combined. Put tablespoons of the mixture onto the prepared baking sheets, spaced well apart.

3. Bake in the preheated oven for 10–12 minutes, or until the cookies are golden brown. Leave to cool on the baking sheet for a few minutes, then transfer the cookies to wire racks to cool completely.

Oaty Raisin & Hazelnut Cookies

Makes 30   Prep Time 15 mins.   Cook Time 12–15 mins.

Ingredients

55 g/2 oz raisins, chopped

125 ml/4 fl oz orange juice

225 g/8 oz butter, softened

140 g/5 oz caster sugar

1 egg yolk, lightly beaten

2 tsp vanilla extract

225 g/8 oz plain flour

55 g/2 oz rolled oats

55 g/2 oz hazelnuts, chopped

salt

whole hazelnuts, to decorate

1. Preheat the oven to 190°C/375°F/Gas Mark 5. Line two baking sheets with baking paper. Put the raisins in a bowl, add the orange ju and leave to soak for 10 minutes.

2. Put the butter and sugar into a bowl and mix well with a wooden spoon, then beat in the egg yolk and vanilla extract. Sift the flour an a pinch of salt into the mixture and add the oats and hazelnuts. Dra the raisins, discarding the orange juice, add them to the mixture and stir until thoroughly combined.

3. Put tablespoons of the mixture onto the prepared baking sheets, spaced well apart. Flatten slightly and place a whole hazelnut in the centre of each cookie. Bake in the preheated oven for 12–15 minute until golden brown. Leave to cool on the baking sheets for a few minutes, then transfer the cookies to wire racks to cool completely.

Black & White Cookies

Makes 20   Prep Time 30 mins.   Cook Time 15 mins.

Ingredients

115 g/4 oz unsalted butter,
plus extra for greasing

1 tsp vanilla extract

175 g/6 oz caster sugar

2 eggs, beaten

300 g/10½ oz plain flour

½ tsp baking powder

200 ml/7 fl oz milk

Icing

225 g/8 oz icing sugar

125 ml/4 fl oz double cream

¼ tsp vanilla extract

75 g/2¾ oz plain chocolate,
broken into pieces

1. Preheat the oven to 190°C/375°F/Gas Mark 5. Grease
baking sheets. Put the butter, vanilla extract and caster sug
a large bowl. Beat the mixture with a whisk until light and
and then beat in the eggs one at a time.

2. Sift the flour and baking powder and fold into the crea
mixture, loosening it with milk as you go until both are use
and the mixture is of dropping consistency.

3. Put tablespoons of the mixture onto the prepared bakin
sheets, spaced well apart. Bake in the preheated oven for
15 minutes, until golden brown. Leave to cool on the bakin
sheets for a few minutes, then transfer the cookies to wire r
to cool completely.

4. To make the icing, put the icing sugar in a bowl and mix
half the cream and the vanilla extract. The consistency sho
be thick but spreadable. Using a palette knife, spread half c
each cookie with white icing. Now, melt the chocolate in a
heatproof bowl over a pan of gently simmering water. Rem
from the heat and stir in the remaining cream. Spread the c
icing over the uncoated cookie halves. Leave to set.

28

3.

4.

Peanut Butter Cookies

Makes 26   Prep Time 15 mins.   Cook Time 12 mins.

Ingredients

115 g/4 oz butter, softened,
plus extra for greasing

115 g/4 oz crunchy peanut butter

115 g/4 oz golden caster sugar

115 g/4 oz light muscovado sugar

1 egg, beaten

1/2 tsp vanilla extract

85 g/3 oz plain flour

1/2 tsp bicarbonate of soda

1/2 tsp baking powder

pinch of salt

115 g/4 oz rolled oats

1. Preheat the oven to 180°C/350°F/Gas Mark 4, then grease three baking sheets.

2. Put the butter and peanut butter in a bowl and beat together. Beat in the caster sugar and muscovado sugar, then gradually beat in the egg and the vanilla extract. Sift the flour, bicarbonate of soda, baking powder and salt into the mixture, add the oats and stir until just combined.

3. Put tablespoons of the mixture onto the prepared baking sheets spaced well apart. Flatten slightly with a fork. Bake in the preheated oven for 12 minutes, until golden brown. Leave to cool on the baking sheets for a few minutes, then transfer the cookies to wire racks to cool completely.

Crunchy Nut & Honey Sandwich Cookies

Makes 30   Prep Time 15 mins.   Cook Time 10–15 mins.

Ingredients

300 g/10½ oz butter, softened

140 g/5 oz caster sugar

1 egg yolk, lightly beaten

2 tsp vanilla extract

280 g/10 oz plain flour

40 g/1½ oz macadamia nuts,
cashew nuts or pine kernels,
chopped

85 g/3 oz icing sugar

85 g/3 oz clover or other set honey

salt

1. Preheat the oven to 190°C/375°F/Gas Mark 5. Line two bakin
sheets with baking paper.

2. Put 225 g/8 oz of the butter and the caster sugar into a bowl an
mix well with a wooden spoon, then beat in the egg yolk and vanill
extract. Sift the flour and a pinch of salt into the mixture and stir
thoroughly combined.

3. Scoop up tablespoons of the mixture and roll into balls. Put hal
them on a prepared baking sheet spaced well apart and flatten gen
Spread out the nuts in a shallow dish and dip one side of the remai
dough balls into them, then place on the other baking sheet nut-sic
up, and flatten gently.

4. Bake in the preheated oven for 10–15 minutes, until golden bro
Leave to cool on the baking sheets for a few minutes, then transfer
cookies to wire racks to cool completely.

5. Beat the remaining butter with the icing sugar and honey until
creamy and thoroughly combined. Spread the honey mixture over
plain cookies and top with the nut-coated cookies.

Snickerdoodles

Makes 40   Prep Time 20 mins. plus chilling   Cook Time 10–12 mins.

Ingredients

225 g/8 oz butter, softened

140 g/5 oz caster sugar

2 large eggs, lightly beaten

1 tsp vanilla extract

400 g/14 oz plain flour

1 tsp bicarbonate of soda

1/2 tsp freshly grated nutmeg

55 g/2 oz pecan nuts,
finely chopped

salt

Cinnamon coating

1 tbsp caster sugar

2 tbsp ground cinnamon

1. Put the butter and sugar into a bowl and mix well with a wooden spoon, then beat in the eggs and vanilla extract. Sift the flour, bicarbonate of soda, nutmeg and a pinch of salt into the mixture, add the pecan nuts and stir until thoroughly combined. Shape the dough into a ball, wrap in clingfilm and chill in the refrigerator for 30–60 minutes.

2. Preheat the oven to 190°C/375°F/Gas Mark 5. Line three baking sheets with baking paper.

3. For the cinnamon coating, mix together the caster sugar and cinnamon in a shallow dish. Scoop up tablespoons of the mixture and roll into balls. Roll each ball in the cinnamon mixture to coat and place on the prepared baking sheets, spaced well apart.

4. Bake in the preheated oven for 10–12 minutes, until golden brown. Leave to cool on the baking sheets for a few minutes, then transfer the cookies to wire racks to cool completely.

Blueberry & Cranberry Cinnamon Cookies

Makes 30   Prep Time 20 mins.   Cook Time 10–15 mins.

Ingredients

225 g/8 oz butter, softened

140 g/5 oz caster sugar

1 egg yolk, lightly beaten

2 tsp vanilla extract

280 g/10 oz plain flour

1 tsp ground cinnamon

55 g/2 oz dried blueberries

55 g/2 oz dried cranberries

55 g/2 oz pine kernels, chopped

salt

1. Preheat the oven to 190°C/375°F/Gas Mark 5. Line two bakin sheets with baking paper.

2. Put the butter and sugar into a bowl and mix well with a wood spoon, then beat in the egg yolk and vanilla extract. Sift the flour, cinnamon and a pinch of salt into the mixture, add the blueberrie cranberries and stir until thoroughly combined.

3. Spread out the pine kernels in a shallow dish. Scoop up tablesp of the mixture and roll them into balls. Roll the balls in the pine kernels to coat, then place on the prepared baking sheets spaced v apart, and flatten slightly.

4. Bake in the preheated oven for 10–15 minutes, until golden br Leave to cool on the baking sheets for a few minutes, then transfe cookies to wire racks to cool completely.

Sliced & Baked Cookies

Sometimes called 'refrigerator' or 'ice box' cookies, this type of cookie dough is shaped into a log or square then chilled until firm before slicing and baking. The dough will keep for up to a week in the refrigerator so you can have freshly baked cookies whenever you want!

Orange & Hazelnut Refrigerator Cookies

Makes 32   Prep Time 40 mins. plus chilling   Cook Time 10–15 mins.

Ingredients

100 g/3½ oz butter, softened, plus extra for greasing

140 g/5 oz caster sugar

1 tsp finely grated orange zest

1 egg, beaten

225 g/8 oz plain flour, sifted

40 g/1½ oz chopped, roasted hazelnuts

Icing

115 g/4 oz icing sugar, sifted

5 tsp fresh orange juice

1. Put the butter, sugar and orange zest into a bowl and beat together until creamy, then gradually beat in the egg. Stir in half the flour and mix to a soft paste, then add the remaining flour and the nuts, and mix to a smooth dough.

2. Shape the dough into a 25-cm/10-inch roll and wrap in clingfilm. Chill for 3–4 hours, occasionally rolling the wrapped dough on a flat surface to ensure a good round shape. Preheat the oven to 190°C/375°F/Gas Mark 5. Grease two large baking sheets with butter.

3. Slice the dough into 32 rounds and place on the prepared baking sheets, spaced well apart. Bake in the preheated oven for 10–15 minutes, until golden around the edges. Leave the cookies to cool on the baking sheets for a few minutes, then transfer to a wire rack to cool completely.

4. To make the icing, beat the sugar and orange juice together in a bowl until smooth. Spoon into a paper piping bag, snip the end and pipe zig-zag lines of icing over each cookie. Leave to set.

3.

4.

Chocolate Squares

Makes 25 | Prep Time 50 mins. plus chilling | Cook Time 12–15 mins.

Ingredients

115 g/4 oz butter, softened,
plus extra for greasing

175 g/6 oz caster sugar

1 large egg, beaten

225 g/8 oz plain flour

25 g/1 oz cocoa powder

1/2 tsp baking powder

Icing

70 g/2 1/2 oz icing sugar

2 tbsp cocoa powder

5–6 tsp milk

1 tbsp white chocolate sprinkles

1 tbsp hundreds and thousands

1. Put the butter and sugar into a bowl and beat together u
creamy, then gradually beat in the egg. Sift in the flour, coc
powder and baking powder, and blend together with a woo
spoon to form a dough. Lightly knead until smooth.

2. Shape the dough into a square log 20 cm/8 inches long
wrap in clingfilm. Chill for 3–4 hours, re-shaping after one
hour. Grease two baking sheets with butter. Preheat the ove
to 180°C/350°F/Gas Mark 4.

3. Slice the dough into 25 squares and place on the prepar
baking sheets, spaced well apart. Bake in the preheated ove
12–15 minutes, until set. Leave to cool on the baking sheets
a few minutes, then transfer to a wire rack to cool complete

4. To make the icing, sift the sugar and cocoa powder into
a bowl and stir in the milk to make a smooth, thick icing. U
a small palette knife to spread the icing over the cookies, th
top with the white chocolate sprinkles and the hundreds an
thousands. Leave to set.

Halloween Pumpkin Cookies

| Makes 30 | Prep Time 30 mins. plus chilling | Cook Time 15 mins. |

Ingredients

100 g/3½ oz butter, softened, plus extra for greasing

55 g/2 oz caster sugar

1 egg, beaten

225 g/8 oz plain flour

25 g/1 oz cornflour

1½ tsp mixed spice

To decorate

350 g/12 oz orange ready-to-roll icing

icing sugar, for dusting

tube of green writing icing

1. Put the butter and sugar into a bowl and beat together until creamy, then gradually beat in the egg. Sift in the flour, cornflour and mixed spice and beat together to form a rough dough. Gather together with your hands and lightly knead until smooth.

2. Shape the dough into a 15-cm/6-inch roll and wrap in clingfilm. Chill for 3–4 hours, occasionally rolling the wrapped dough on a flat surface to ensure a good round shape. Preheat the oven to 180°C/350°F/Gas Mark 4. Grease two large baking sheets with butter.

3. Thinly slice the dough into 30 rounds and place on the prepared baking sheets, spaced well apart. Bake in the preheated oven for 15 minutes, until golden brown. Leave to cool on the baking sheets for a few minutes, then transfer to wire rack to cool completely.

4. Thinly roll out the orange icing on a work surface lightly dusted with icing sugar. Use a pumpkin-shaped cutter to stamp out 30 pumpkins, re-rolling the icing as necessary. Use the writing icing to attach the pumpkins to each cookie and to pipe on stalks and leaves. Using the tip of a sharp knife, score vertical curved lines in the orange icing. Leave to set.

45

Birthday Cookies

Makes 24   Prep Time 30 mins. plus chilling   Cook Time 12–15 minutes

Ingredients

115 g/4 oz butter, softened,
plus extra for greasing

140 g/5 oz caster sugar

1 egg, beaten

1/2 tsp vanilla extract

250 g/9 oz plain flour

To decorate

1 quantity royal icing (see page 5)

85 g/3 oz each pink, blue and
yellow ready-to-roll icing

icing sugar, for dusting

tube of red writing icing

1. Put the butter and sugar into a bowl and beat together until creamy. Gradually beat in the egg and vanilla extract. Sift in flour and blend with a wooden spoon to form a rough dough. Lightly knead until smooth.

2. Shape the dough into a square log 20 cm/8 inches long and wrap in clingfilm. Chill for 3–4 hours, re-shaping after one hour. Grease two baking sheets with butter. Preheat the oven to 180°C/350°F/Gas Mark 4.

3. Slice the dough into 24 squares and place on the prepared baking sheets, spaced well apart. Bake in the preheated oven 12–15 minutes, until pale golden in colour. Leave to cool on baking sheets for a few minutes, then transfer to a wire rack cool completely.

4. Beat a few drops of water into the royal icing to give a spooning consistency. Spread the icing on the cookies. Thinly roll out the ready-to-roll icing on a work surface lightly dusted with icing sugar and cut out parcels, cupcakes and balloons. Place the shapes on the cookies and pipe ribbons, cherries and string with the writing icing. Leave to set.

3.

4.

Biscotti

Makes 30   Prep Time 20 mins. plus chilling   Cook Time 10 mins.

Ingredients

225 g/8 oz butter, softened

140 g/5 oz caster sugar

finely grated rind of 1 lemon

1 egg yolk, lightly beaten

2 tsp brandy

280 g/10 oz plain flour

85 g/3 oz pistachio nuts

salt

icing sugar, for dusting

1. Put the butter, sugar and lemon rind into a bowl and mix well with a wooden spoon, then beat in the egg yolk and brandy. Sift the flour and a pinch of salt into the mixture, stir the pistachio nuts, and mix until thoroughly combined. Shape the mixture into a log, flatten slightly, wrap in clingfilm and chill in the refrigerator for 30–60 minutes.

2. Preheat the oven to 190°C/375°F/Gas Mark 5. Line two baking sheets with baking paper.

3. Unwrap the dough and cut it slightly on the diagonal into 5-mm/¼-inch slices with a sharp serrated knife. Put them on the prepared baking sheets, spaced well apart.

4. Bake in the preheated oven for 10 minutes, until golden brown. Leave to cool on the baking sheets for a few minutes then transfer the cookies to wire racks to cool completely. Dust with icing sugar.

Blueberry & Orange Cookies

Makes 30   Prep Time 25 mins. plus chilling   Cook Time 10–15 mins.

Ingredients

225 g/8 oz butter, softened

140 g/5 oz caster sugar

1 egg yolk, lightly beaten

1 tsp orange extract

280 g/10 oz plain flour

100 g/3½ oz dried blueberries

100 g/3½ oz cream cheese

grated rind of 1 orange

40 g/1½ oz macadamia nuts, finely chopped

salt

1. Put the butter and sugar into a bowl and mix well with a wooden spoon, then beat in the egg yolk and orange extrac. Sift the flour and a pinch of salt into the mixture, add the blueberries and stir until thoroughly combined. Shape the dough into a log, wrap in clingfilm and chill in the refrigera for 30–60 minutes.

2. Preheat the oven to 190°C/375°F/Gas Mark 5. Line two baking sheets with baking paper.

3. Unwrap the dough and cut into 5-mm/¼-inch slices with sharp serrated knife. Put them on the prepared baking shee spaced well apart.

4. Bake for 10–15 minutes, until golden brown. Leave to co on the baking sheets for 5–10 minutes, then using a palette knife, carefully transfer to wire racks to cool completely.

5. Just before serving, beat the cream cheese in a bowl and in the orange rind. Spread the mixture over the cookies an sprinkle with the chopped nuts.

3.

5.

Pressed & Piped Cookies

These cookies are made with sweet soft dough, which can be shaped by piping from a large piping bag with a fluted nozzle or with a special cookie press. They have a lovely light and crisp texture and you can experiment with different shapes and patterns.

Viennese Fingers

Makes 16 Prep Time 20 mins. Cook Time 10–15 mins.

Ingredients

100 g/3¹/₂ oz unsalted butter, plus extra for greasing

25 g/1 oz golden caster sugar

¹/₂ tsp vanilla extract

100 g/3¹/₂ oz self-raising flour

100 g/3¹/₂ oz plain chocolate

1. Preheat the oven to 160°C/325°F/Gas Mark 3. Lightly grease two baking sheets.

2. Place the butter, sugar and vanilla extract in a bowl and cream together until pale and fluffy. Stir in the flour, mixing evenly to a fairly stiff dough.

3. Place the mixture in a piping bag fitted with a large star nozzle and pipe about 16 fingers, each 6 cm/2¹/₂ inches long onto the prepared baking sheets spaced well apart.

4. Bake in the preheated oven for 10–15 minutes, until golden brown. Leave to cool on the baking sheets for a few minutes then transfer the cookies to wire racks to cool completely.

5. Place the chocolate in a small heatproof bowl set over a pan of gently simmering water until melted. Remove from the heat. Dip the ends of each biscuit into the chocolate to coat, then place on a sheet of baking paper and leave to set.

Chocolate Wreaths

Makes 16   Prep Time 15 mins.   Cook Time 15–20 mins.

Ingredients

125 g/4½ oz butter, softened,
plus extra for greasing
40 g/1½ oz icing sugar
125 g/4½ oz plain flour
25 g/1 oz cornflour
15 g/½ oz cocoa powder
½ tsp vanilla extract

Icing

100 g/3½ oz icing sugar
2 tsp cocoa powder
2 tbsp milk

1. Preheat the oven to 180°C/350°F/Gas Mark 4. Grease baking sheets.

2. Put the butter and icing sugar in a bowl and beat togeth until pale and creamy. Sift over the flour, cornflour and co powder and beat well until smooth and creamy. Beat in th vanilla extract.

3. Spoon the mixture into a large piping bag fitted with a star nozzle and pipe 16 x 7-cm/2¾-inch diameter circles the prepared baking sheets.

4. Bake in the preheated oven for 15–20 minutes until just Leave to cool on the baking sheets for 5 minutes then trans to a wire rack to cool completely.

5. To make the icing, sift the icing sugar and cocoa powde a bowl and beat in the milk to make a smooth thin icing. G dip the top of each cookie into the icing. Leave to set.

Cherry & Almond Flower Cookies

Makes 45   Prep Time 30 mins.   Cook Time 8–10 mins.

Ingredients

115 g/4 oz butter, softened
85 g/3 oz sugar
1 egg yolk
few drops almond extract
150 g/5½ oz plain flour
12 glacé cherries, quartered

Icing

115 g/4 oz icing sugar
1½–2 tbsp lukewarm water

1. Preheat the oven to 190°C/375°F/Gas Mark 5.

2. Put the butter and sugar into a bowl and beat with a hand-held electric mixer until pale and creamy. Beat in the egg yolk and almond extract, then stir in the flour. Mix to a soft dough.

3. Use a cookie press fitted with a flower disc to stamp out 45 cookies onto two to three cold, non-stick baking sheets (refilling the press when necessary). Alternatively, roll the dough into small balls and flatten gently onto the baking sheets. Place a cherry quarter in the centre of each cookie.

4. Bake in the preheated oven for 8–10 minutes, until just golden around the edges. Leave to cool on the baking sheets a few minutes, then transfer to a wire rack to cool completely.

5. To make the icing, sift the sugar into a bowl and stir in enough of the water to make a smooth, runny icing. Brush over the cookies and leave to set.

Lemon Iced Cookies

Makes 45   Prep Time 30 mins.   Cook Time 8–10 mins.

Ingredients

115 g/4 oz butter, softened
85 g/3 oz sugar
1 egg yolk
1 tsp finely grated lemon zest
150 g/5½ oz plain flour

Icing

150 g/5½ oz icing sugar
1 tbsp lukewarm water
1 tbsp lemon juice
pink and yellow food colouring

1. Preheat the oven to 190°C/375°F/Gas Mark 5.

2. Put the butter and sugar into a bowl and beat with a woo[d]
spoon until pale and creamy. Beat in the egg yolk and lemo[n]
zest, then stir in the flour. Mix to a soft dough.

3. Use a cookie press fitted with a disc of your choice to sta[mp]
out 45 cookies onto two to three cold, non-stick baking she[ets]
(re-filling the press when necessary). Alternatively, roll the
dough into small balls or shapes of your choice and flatten
gently onto the baking sheets.

4. Bake in the preheated oven for 8–10 minutes, until golde[n]
around the edges. Leave to cool on the baking sheets for a f[ew]
minutes, then transfer to a wire rack to cool completely.

5. To make the icing, sift the icing sugar into a bowl and sti[r]
in the water and lemon juice to make a smooth icing. Colou[r]
one half of the icing pink and the other half yellow. Spoon [into]
paper piping bags, snip the ends and pipe decorations on th[e]
cookies. Leave to set.

3.

5.

Melting Moments

Makes 32   Prep Time 20 mins.   Cook Time 15–20 mins.

Ingredients

350 g/12 oz unsalted butter,
softened

85 g/3 oz icing sugar

1/2 tsp vanilla extract

300 g/10 1/2 oz plain flour

50 g/1 3/4 oz cornflour

1. Preheat the oven to 180°C/350°F/Gas Mark 4. Line two large baking sheets with baking paper.

2. Place the butter and icing sugar in a large bowl and beat together until light and fluffy, then beat in the vanilla extract. Sift in the flour and cornflour and mix thoroughly.

3. Spoon the mixture into a piping bag fitted with a large star nozzle and pipe cookies onto the prepared baking sheets, spaced well apart.

4. Bake in the preheated oven for 15–20 minutes, until golden brown. Leave to cool on the baking sheets for a few minutes, then transfer the cookies to wire racks to cool completely.